Mrs. Feeny

and the

Grubby Garden Gang

Sandy Baker
Illustrated by Jim DeWitt

Black Garnet Press
Santa Rosa, California

In Memory of Lindsay

Acknowledgments

For all his support and encouragement, thanks go to my number one fan, my husband Bud Metzger. And many thanks also go to three organizations, for different reasons, that helped me reach this place of publishing Mrs. Feeny: the Sonoma County Master Gardeners; the Redwood Writers branch of the California Writers Club; and the Bay Area Independent Publishers Assn., and its president and my book designer Pete Masterson. And of course, thanks go to my new friend and illustrator Jim DeWitt.

Text copyright © 2011 by Sandy Baker

Illustrations copyright © 2011 by Jim Dewitt

All rights reserved. No part of this publication may be reproduced, stored in a retrieval system, or transmitted in any form or by any means, graphic, electronic, mechanical, photocopying, taping, recording, or otherwise, without the written permission of the author, except in the case of brief quotations embodied in critical articles and reviews.

ISBN 978-0-9911790-0-8

Published by
Black Garnet Press
P.O. Box 2914
Santa Rosa CA 95405

Visit the author's web site for more information: www.sandybakerwriter.com

Printed in the United States of America

"You kids get off my lawn," screamed Mrs. Feeny, running out her front door. "Walk on the sidewalk like normal human beings!"

"Meany Mrs. Feeny, Witchy Widow Feeny," the boys sang, scattering.

Around the corner, Buddy, Josh, and Brad laughed. "Whew, we made it across again!" Buddy said. "It's a great dirt short-cut, isn't it? Ha, ha, ha."

"Remember when she put that stupid fence along the edge—it was so easy to jump?" said Josh. "Then she put in those dumb rocks. Heck, that didn't stop us either."

"Nah! And when she put up a No Trespassing sign, we flipped it backwards?" laughed Brad. "She even turned on the sprinkler, and I rode my bike through! Cool."

"She's a mean, cranky old lady," Buddy said. "Creepy, too—she must watch us out her window. And what a water-waster! But I don't care 'cause then we can splash through it when it runs onto the sidewalk and slide around when it's muddy."

"One time, didn't she say she would call the police?" asked Brad. "What, are the police gonna arrest us for cutting across her lawn?"

Then one day as the three boys walked back from school, they saw Mrs. Feeny out front digging up her lawn, humming to herself. Clumps of grass were in a pile.

"Buddy, go talk to her," egged on Josh. "Find out what she's doing."

"No way, you go," said Buddy. "She's too mean. Double-dog-dare you, Brad, you're brave."

"Okay, Okay. Umm, what-cha doin', Mrs. Feeny," Brad asked. "You gonna wreck the path?"

"No," she replied. "Want to help? Want to get *really* dirty?" It was May and she needed to get this digging done.

"Gee, I don't know," he said, "but what-cha doin'?"

"You'll see…"

"What she's up to?" Buddy asked. "I wonder if she's doing something scary?"

"Holy cow, is she digging a grave?" Josh wondered. "Maybe she buried someone already. She could be dangerous."

"Wait," said Buddy. "She's right in the front yard—cars and people go by. If we're there together, we can protect each other. We'll just run or yell if she tries anything."

The next day, Buddy, Brad, and Josh showed up and looked around.

"Yeah, me and Brad and Josh are here to help," Buddy announced to Mrs. Feeny. "We know how to dig really good. Are you looking for treasure?"

"Certainly not," she said. "Young men, I'd like you to dig up all the grass, but be sure you leave the path alone."

"Okay. Hey, guys, this is kinda fun. See, we're safe so far," Josh whispered as Brad and Buddy threw dirt clods at each other.

"Wow, look at the cherry brownies," said Brad as Mrs. Feeny brought out a tray. "Do you think they're poison?" he whispered to Josh.

"Nah. Boy, they look good," Josh said. "Let's try 'em." Dirty hands and all, the three gobbled up even the crumbs.

The day after, a very much alive Buddy announced, "Hey, Mrs. Feeny, we brought Kelly and Sara. They know how to dig, too."

"You kids are doing a fine job," she told them. "I appreciate it. I need to get this done very soon."

"Okay, but you haven't told us what-cha doin'," Brad said.

"You'll see…"

Next day when the same five appeared, Mrs. Feeny said, "Please use the wheelbarrow to take the grass clumps to my compost pile in back."

A dump truck delivered a big load of dark, yucky something. "Eeeew, what's that smell?" asked the kids. "Eeeew."

"It's steer manure mixed in with the compost," Mrs. Feeny explained. "It's just decomposed grass, yard waste, and manure. It lightens up the soil so water, air, and plant roots can get through."

Mrs. Feeny and the kids spent the day digging the compost into the soil, raking it smooth—but not the path.

Next day another truck dumped a load of mulch.

"Okay, kids, spread these wood chips onto the pathway, neat and even. Once you're finished, you have my permission to use it any time you want—*only* the path."

"Yay!"

18

"Oh yum, look at these lemon bars," said Kelly. "Our favorite, Mrs. Feeny. Do you care if we're dirty and sweaty when we eat this stuff?"

"Oh my, no. I think I'll name you the Grubby Gang!" laughed Mrs. Feeny.

"Okay! But what-cha gonna do with the yard now?" Sara asked, puzzled.

"I'm going to plant a garden. Want to help?" she asked. "It'll be a smelly-touchy-foody garden."

"A what?" they asked in unison.

"A smelly-touchy-foody garden," Mrs. Feeny said. "No more lawn. It uses too much water."

Josh repeated, "A smelly-touchy-foody garden. Yeah!" They sang it over and over.

"Now you better call us the Grubby *Garden* Gang," giggled Kelly.

"We have to plant before the summer heat. These little seedlings are already strong," Mrs. Feeny pointed out. "Some called annuals last only 'til the first frost, and the others called perennials grow year after year."

The kids planted sunflowers and hollyhocks near the house, and some sweet peas and beans on strings at the fence. They put in daisies and cosmos, zinnias, marigolds, snapdragons, and wildflowers. Next they added some tomatoes, zucchini, watermelon, and pumpkins. And last, they planted the herbs parsley, mint, thyme, and oregano.

"Some of these smell real good, some feel funny to touch, and some we can eat," she told the Grubby Garden Gang. "And many use hardly any water at all. No sprays or chemicals either."

"Wow, we dig this," they echoed each other. "Get it? Dig? Ha ha ha."

"We'll help you water and weed the garden, Mrs. Feeny," Josh announced. "We'll take turns, okay?"

"Look at the tiny plants popping up—almost every day," Sara exclaimed a week later.

By the end of July, the garden was flourishing.

"Mrs. Feeny isn't so bad after all, is she," Buddy whispered. "We can touch and smell the flowers and even take home some tomatoes and squash. Oh boy, just wait 'til the watermelons get ripe!"

"So many butterflies and bugs are here now," said Josh. "Look, a hummingbird."

"This is Mrs. Feeny's Smelly-Touchy-Foody Garden," Buddy and the Grubby Garden Gang announced to anyone who stopped by.

"No, Gang, this is **our** Smelly-Touchy-Foody Garden!" Mrs. Feeny said, as they all cheered.

Mrs. Feeny's Garden Glossary

Annual—a flower or plant that lives for only one year or less. It is planted after the last frost in the spring and very often dies with the first hard frost in late fall or winter.

Compost—a brown or black dirt-like substance made from decomposed organic matter like grass clippings, dead flowers, leaves or kitchen waste (lettuce, potato peels, coffee grounds, but no meat, cheese or oils).

Compost Pile—the area where you pile up all the materials to create compost; you water and stir it around, too, to help it decompose faster. Some people make enclosures made out of boards or wire.

Decompose—a process where your yard and kitchen waste break down, decay and rot to form compost. Heat and moisture speed it up.

Herbs—plants that can be used for cooking; they smell good and taste good. Some herbs are thyme, rosemary, oregano, sage, and parsley.

Manure—animal waste; many manures, like steer, horse, chicken, and rabbit, can be added to compost piles. Never add dog waste.

Mulch—living (bark, straw, leaves, sawdust) or non-living (gravel, marble chips, shells) material spread on soil around plants or on pathways. Smaller bark chips and gravel can be walked on. Mulch can stop weeds from growing and keep water in the soil. It makes a garden look nice and neat.

Perennial—a plant (not woody like a tree) or flower that lives for more than a couple of years. In winter, while the top will die, the roots still live, and the plant grows again the next season.

Seedling—a small, young plant, grown from a seed; they often come in plastic six-packs.

Yard waste—leaves, grass clippings, dead flowers, plant trimmings; all can be added to a compost pile. It is never a good idea to add weeds.

About the Author

Sandy Baker writes, gardens, and crafts. She's a contributing writer to *Travel Host* magazine and editor/consultant for an international thriller being released in 2012.

Sandy began her career as a technical writer and editor, followed by teaching English to Army G.I.s in Germany. She was a newspaper reporter and columnist in New Jersey and later had a long career as a university fundraiser and publicist in Southern California. Her greatest pleasure these days is writing short stories for children and poetry for and about teens.

A Master Gardener since 2000, she writes for the MG website and lectures in N. California on basic landscape design, lawn alternatives, drought tolerant gardening, and use of native plants.

She lives in Sonoma County with her husband and dog on their flower-packed, nearly lawnless property. Visit www.sandybakerwriter.com for related articles and kid fun. Sandy has a degree in English from Penn State.

About the Illustrator

Jim DeWitt was born in Oakland, California, in 1930.

As a five-year-old, he drew pictures of the sailboat his father was building in their backyard, and dreamed of someday being her skipper. After high school, he studied art for six years at the California College of Arts and Crafts and Los Angeles Art Center — learning sailmaking and racing sailboats in his spare time.

In addition to shows and exhibitions in San Diego, San Francisco, New York, Waikiki and Newport, Rhode Island, Jim has exhibited in galleries and museums worldwide. Jim's racing paintings are valued assets in private and corporate collections, and are on permanent display in many yacht clubs.

Today, Jim is happiest painting colorful, joyful subject matter that tells a story. His work can be seen on his website, www.jimdewitt.com and at DeWitt Gallery and Framing in Point Richmond, California.

www.ingramcontent.com/pod-product-compliance
Lightning Source LLC
Chambersburg PA
CBHW042127040426
42450CB00002B/108